MORE LAUGH -OUT- LOUD JOKES for KIDS

ROB ELLIOTT

SPIRE

© 2014 by Robert E. Teigen

Published by Revell
a division of Baker Publishing Group
P.O. Box 6287, Grand Rapids, MI 49516-6287
www.revellbooks.com

ISBN 978-0-8007-8821-6

Printed in the United States of America

16   17   18   19   20   21   13   12   11

Books by Rob Elliott

MORE LAUGH OUT LOUD JOKES for KIDS

Knock knock.

Who's there?

Chew.

Chew who?

I want to hang out with chew so let me in!

Mark: **What's the best place to chop down a Christmas tree?**

Tim: I'm not sure.

Mark: **About three inches off the ground.**

Q: Why did the broccoli slap the lettuce?

A: Because it was being fresh!

Q: Why did the elephants take up the least amount of room on Noah's ark?

A: Because they kept everything in their trunks!

Q: Why did the moon feel sick to its stomach?

A: It was a full moon.

Suzy: I'm so smart I can sing the whole alphabet song!

Jimmy: That's nothing. I can sing it in lower case and capitals!

Q: Why were the lamb and goat such good friends?

A: Because they had a very close relation-sheep.

Q: What do you get when you spill your coffee in the dirt?

A: Coffee grounds!

Q: What kind of vegetable has the worst manners?

A: A rude-abaga.

Q: What is penguin's favorite kind of food?

A: Ice-burgers.

Q: What do you get when you brush your teeth with dish soap?

A: Bubble gums.

Q: What kind of trees wear mittens?

A: Palm trees.

Q: Why was the library so busy?

A: It was overbooked.

Q: What do you get when you cross a porcupine with a snail?

A: A slowpoke.

Q: When do farmers go bald?

A: When they have re-seeding hairlines.

Q: How do you know when it's been raining cats and dogs?

A: When you step in a poodle.

Justin: Do you know how to make a pineapple shake?

Nate: You mix pineapple, milk, and ice cream?

Justin: No, you take it to a scary movie!

Q: What do you get when you cross an owl and bubble gum?

A: A bird that will chews wisely.

Knock knock.

Who's there?

Leon.

Leon who?

I'd be Leon if I told you I didn't love knock-knock jokes!

Q: **What kind of homework do you do on the couch?**

A: Multipli-cushion.

Tim: **Did you hear about the guy who stuck his finger in a light socket?**

Scott: No, what happened?

Tim: **It was shocking!**

Q: How does a cow get to the office?

A: On a cow-moo-ter train.

Q: What do you get when you cross a dinosaur and gunpowder?

A: Dino-mite.

Q: Why shouldn't you stare at the turkey dressing at Thanksgiving?

A: The turkey will be embarrassed.

Q: Why did the skeleton refuse to go to the dance?

A: He had no-body to dance with.

Q: Why did the suspenders have to go to jail?

A: They held up a pair of pants.

Q: Why don't fish ever get a summer vacation?

A: They spend every day in schools.

Q: What do you get when you play tug-of-war with a pig?

A: Pulled pork.

Joe: Can you believe that I ate six helpings of spaghetti last night?

Bill: Well, I wouldn't put it pasta!

Q: Why did the orange have to stop and take a nap?

A: It ran out of juice.

Q: What do you call a boomerang that won't come back to you?

A: A stick.

Q: Did you hear about the new restaurant they put on Mars?

A: I hear the food is out of this world.

Q: How much did Santa pay for his reindeer?

A: Just a few bucks. They didn't cost him much doe.

Q: What is a trumpet player's favorite month of the year?

A: March.

Sally: What is a mummy's favorite kind of music?

Bill: I'm not sure.

Sally: Wrap music!

Q: Why couldn't the fish go shopping?

A: It didn't have anemone.

Andrew: Do you know how to spell "hard water" using only three letters?

Dave: I'm pretty sure that's impossible!

Andrew: No, it isn't. I-C-E is hard water!

Q: What kind of motorcycle do bulls like to ride?

A: They ride a Cow-asaki.

Q: What does a grizzly do on a hard day?

A: He'll just grin and bear it.

Q: How many months have 28 days?

A: All twelve of them do!

Knock knock.

Who's there?

Bean.

Bean who?

Its bean way too long since you've heard a knock-knock joke!

Q: What do you call a pumpkin that watches over you?

A: A body-gourd.

Q: What do you call a greasy bug?

A: A butter-fly.

Q: Why did the whale cross the ocean?

A: To get to the other tide.

Q: Why did the rabbit need to relax?

A: He was feeling jumpy.

Q: Why did the skunk cross the road?

A: To get to the odor side!

Q: What do you get when you combine an elephant and a skunk?

A: A smell-ephant.

Q: What kind of vegetable is hip and cool?

A: A radish.

Q: How do you sneak across the desert without being seen?

A: You wear camel-flage.

Q: What is a maple's favorite class at school?

A: Geometree.

Knock knock.

Who's there?

Arthur.

Arthur who?

Arthur any more funny knock-knock jokes?

Q: Why wouldn't the turkey eat any pumpkin pie?

A: It was too stuffed.

Q: What do you call bears with no ears?

A: B!

Q: What happened when the turkey got in a fight?

A: He got the stuffing knocked out of him.

Knock knock.

Who's there?

Annie.

Annie who?

Annie chance I could tell you another knock-knock joke?

Q: What does a black belt eat for lunch?

A: Kung food!

Q: Why did the lobster get grounded by his parents?

A: He was always getting himself in hot water!

Q: What kind of automobile is the same going backward and forward?

A: Racecar.

Knock knock.

Who's there?

Gus.

Gus who?

I bet you can't Gus who this is!

Q: What did the skunks do on Saturday night?

A: They watched a movie on their smell-evision.

Q: What do you call bunny's prized possessions?

A: Hare-looms.

Q: What do you get when you combine a kitty and a fish?

A: A purr-anha!

Q: What do fish like to sing during the holidays?

A: Christmas corals.

Q: What do you get when you drop a pumpkin from your roof?

A: Squash.

Q: Why did the apples want to hang out with the banana?

A: Because it was so appeeling.

Q: Why couldn't the skeletons play any music?

A: They didn't have any organs.

Adel: My math book fell into my jack-o'-lantern the other day.

Anna: What did you do?

Adel: I made pumpkin pi.

Q: What did the blackbird use to get the door open?

A: A crow bar!

Q: What do you call kids who play outside in the snow?

A: Chilled-ren.

Q: What did the almond say to the psychiatrist?

A: "Everybody says I'm nuts!"

Q: Why was the skeleton laughing?

A: Somebody tickled its funny bone.

Q: How do you keep a restaurant safe from criminals?

A: Use a burger alarm.

Q: What does a cat eat for breakfast?

A: Mice Krispies.

Q: How does a pig get to the hospital?

A: In a ham-bulance.

Q: What do you get when you cross a dog and broccoli?

A: Collie-flower.

Q: What language do pigs speak?

A: French, because they go "Oui, oui, oui," all the way home!

Q: What has a head and a tail, but no body?

A: A penny.

Q: What do you feed a teddy bear?

A: Stuffing!

Q: Why did the elf get in trouble with his teacher?

A: He didn't do his gnomework.

Q: What do you get when you cross a snake with dessert?

A: A pie-thon.

Dave: What do you get when you cross an airplane, a car, and a cat?

Bill: I give up.

Dave: A flying car-pet!

Q: What kind of homework do you do in a taxi?

A: Vocabulary.

Q: What has a face and two hands, but no arms or legs?

A: A clock!

Q: How do you make friends with everyone at school?

A: Become the princi-pal.

Q: What do you get when you play basketball in Hawaii?

A: Hula-Hoops!

Q: What is a snowman's favorite cereal?

A: Frosted Flakes.

Q: What do you call a boy with no money in his pocket?

A: Nickel-less.

Q: How did the oyster get to the doctor?

A: In a clam-bulance.

Q: Why was the snake so funny?

A: His jokes were hiss-terical.

Knock knock.
  Who's there?
Whale.
  Whale who?
Whale you let me tell you another knock-knock joke?

Q: What is a sailor's favorite kind of book to read?

A: Ferry tales.

Q: Which word in the dictionary is always spelled wrong?

A: WRONG, of course!

Q: What does a monster put on top of his hot fudge sundae?

A: Whipped scream.

Q: Why did the burglar steal the eggs?

A: He likes his eggs poached!

Q: Why can't you ever trust an atom?

A: They make up everything!

Q: Why did the chef have to stop cooking?

A: He ran out of thyme.

Q: What is an elephant's favorite vegetable?

A: Squash.

Q: How do frogs get the ice off their car windows?

A: They use the defrogger.

Q: How do you know if you have an elephant in your refrigerator?

A: The refrigerator door won't shut!

Q: What did the tornado say to the race car?

A: "Can I take you for a spin?"

Q: What does a weasel like to read?

A: Pop-up books!

Q: What is a squirrel's favorite ballet?

A: The Nutcracker!

Q: How did everyone know that the lion swallowed the bear?

A: His stomach was growling.

Q: What do frogs like with their cheeseburgers?

A: French flies and a croak.

Q: What is the best thing to do with a blue whale?

A: Tell it a joke and cheer it up!

Q: What happened to the dog after it swallowed the watch?

A: It was full of ticks.

Q: What kind of shoes do foxes wear?

A: Sneak-ers.

Q: What did the baker say when his cookie wouldn't crumble?

A: "That's one tough cookie!"

Q: What did the bee say to the flower?

A: "Hi, honey!"

Q: What did the flower say to the bee?

A: "Buzz off!"

Q: What did the picture say when the police showed up?

A: "I didn't do it—I've been framed!"

Q: Why did the king go to the dentist?

A: Because he wanted a crown on his tooth!

Q: Why was the comedian sad?

A: He thought his life was a joke!

Knock knock.

Who's there?

Auto.

Auto who?

You really auto tell me some knock-knock jokes!

Q: Why did the book join the police force?

A: It wanted to go undercover!

Q: What do you get when you cross a bird and a bee?

A: A buzzard.

Q: Why did the elephant quit his job?

A: He was working for peanuts.

Q: What do you get when you throw a couch in the pond?

A: A sitting duck!

Q: What do you get when you cross a horse and a pencil?

A: Horseback writing.

Q: Why did the policeman go to the baseball game?

A: He heard someone had stolen second base.

Q: What kinds of keys are easy to swallow?

A: Cookies.

Knock knock.

Who's there?

Ken.

Ken who?

Ken I tell you another knock-knock joke?

Q: Why did the horse go to the psychiatrist?

A: It was feeling un-stable.

Q: What kind of sea creatures are the most musical?

A: Fish, because they have so many scales!

Q: When do you know a tiger isn't telling the truth?

A: When it's a lion.

Q: Why did the baker go to work every day?

A: He really kneaded the dough!

Q: What did the bumblebee say to his wife?

A: "Honey, you're bee-utiful."

Q: Where does a cow go when it's hungry?

A: To the calf-eteria.

Knock knock.
   Who's there?
Tibet.
   Tibet who?
Early Tibet, early to rise.

Bob: Did you hear about the farmer
      who wrote a joke book?

Bill: No, is it any good?

Bob: The jokes are really corn-y.

Q: What does a moose like to play at parties?

A: Moose-ical chairs.

Q: Who leads the orchestra at the zoo?

A: The boa-conductor.

Q: What did the drum say to the violin?

A: "Stop harping at me!"

Q: What do little cows give?

A: Condensed milk.

Q: What does a possum like to do for fun?

A: Hang out with its friends!

Q: Who helped the mermaid go to the ball?

A: Her fairy cod-mother.

Knock knock.
   Who's there?
Hector.
   Hector who?
When the Hector you going to open the door?

Q: What does a snowman eat for dessert?

A: Ice krispy treats.

Emma: Can February March?

Leah: No, but April May.

Q: **What do you call someone with no body and no nose?**

A: No-body knows.

Q: **Which has more courage, a rock or a tree?**

A: A rock—it's boulder!

Q: **Why did the plant go to the dentist?**

A: It needed a root canal!

Josh: Do you think change is hard?

Joe: I sure do—have you ever tried to bend a quarter?

Patient: Hey doc, I think I broke my leg in two places. What should I do?

Doctor: Don't go to those two places anymore!

Knock knock.

Who's there?

Minnow.

Minnow who?

If you can think of a better knock-knock joke, let minnow.

John: I'm really bright.

Jane: How bright are you?

John: I'm so bright, my mother calls me sun.

Jill: I'm upset that my new toaster isn't waterproof.

Jen: What's so bad about that?

Jill: When I found out, I was shocked!

Q: How do fleas travel from one dog to another?

A: They itchhike their way there!

Q: What is a swan's favorite Christmas carol?

A: Duck the Halls.

Q: Why did the chicken go to bed?

A: It was eggs-hausted.

Knock knock.
> Who's there?

Gas.
> Gas who?

I bet you can't gas who this is at the door!

Q: What is something that has to be broken before you can use it?

A: An egg!

Knock knock.
> Who's there?

Window.
> Window who?

Window you want to hear another great knock-knock joke?

Bill: Do you know who told me you sound like an owl when you talk?

Joe: No, who?

Q: What did the fork say to the butter knife?

A: "You're so dull."

Q: What do you get from an invisible cow?

A: Evaporated milk.

Q: What do you get when you cross a dentist and a boat?

A: A tooth ferry.

Q: Why did the boy eat his homework?

A: The teacher said it would be a piece of cake.

Q: Why did the banana put on sunscreen?

A: It didn't want to peel.

Q: Why did the Starburst go to school?

A: It wanted to be a Smartie.

Patient: Doc, I think I'm turning into a piano.

Doc: Well, that's just grand!

Q: Where do you learn to cut wood?

A: At boarding school.

Q: Where does a volcano wash its hands?

A: In the lava-tory.

Q: Why did the wheel stop turning?

A: It was too tired.

Q: What goes up but doesn't come back down?

A: Your age!

Q: How did the pig write a letter?

A: With a pig pen.

Q: Which giraffe won the race?

A: It was a tie—they were neck and neck the whole time.

Q: What does a pig use when it has a rash?

A: Oinkment.

Q: Why did the tree need to take a nap?

A: It was bushed.

Knock knock.

Who's there?

Pecan.

Pecan who?

You should pecan someone your own size!

Q: What has four wheels and flies?

A: A garbage truck!

Q: What is the worst day of the week for fish?

A: Fryday!

Q: What kind of buttons does everyone wear?

A: Belly buttons.

Q: How do you repair a squashed tomato?

A: Use tomato paste!

Q: What is a soda's favorite subject in school?

A: Fizzics.

Q: What sometimes runs but never walks?

A: Your nose!

Q: What is a cow's favorite painting?

A: The Moona Lisa.

Knock knock.

   Who's there?

Rita.

   Rita who?

Did you Rita good book lately?

Knock knock.
Who's there?
Ears.
Ears who?
Ears looking at you, kid.

Q: What is the best time to see the dentist?

A: At tooth-thirty.

Q: What kind of tree needs a doctor all the time?

A: A sycamore tree.

Q: Why did the bathtub need a vacation?

A: Because it was drained.

Q: What kind of vegetable is lazy and irresponsible?

A: A dead-beet.

Q: Why did the meteorite go to Hollywood?

A: It wanted to be a star.

Q: What do you get when you cross a snow-man and a lion?

A: Frost-bite.

Q: What do you get when you throw noodles in a Jacuzzi?

A: Spa-ghetti.

Q: When is a cow happy, then sad, and then angry?

A: When it's moo-dy.

Q: What did the ocean say to the fishing boat?

A: Nothing—it just waved.

Q: Which of Santa's reindeer has the worst manners?

A: Rude-olph.

Q: Why did the inventor get struck by lightning?

A: He was brain-storming.

Q: What did the one maple leaf say to the other maple leaf?

A: "I'm falling for you!"

Q: Why did the stereo explode?

A: It was radio-active.

Q: How do you know when a bucket is feeling sick?

A: When it looks a little pail.

Q: What plays music on your head?

A: A head-band.

Q: What kind of bird do you have with every meal?

A: A swallow.

Q: What do you call a lion that gives you presents?

A: Santa Claws.

Q: What do you get when you cross a flower, a car, and the USA?

A: A pink car nation.

Q: What did Mrs. Claus say to Santa when he was complaining about the rain on Christmas Eve?

A: "Oh, let it rain, dear."

Q: What's a hyena's favorite kind of cookie?

A: A snickerdoodle.

Q: Why can't a beaver use a computer?

A: It doesn't know how to log in.

Q: What do you call your dog when it goes deaf?

A: It doesn't matter—it can't hear you anyway!

Q: How much did Santa's sleigh cost?

A: Nothing—it was on the house!

Q: What is a skeleton's favorite instrument?

A: A trombone.

Q: Why didn't the panda bear get the job?

A: It didn't have the right koala-fications.

Sally: Can you believe I gave my pigs a bath?

Susie: That's a bunch of hog wash!

Q: Why did the clock go back four seconds?

A: It was really hungry!

Q: Why did the lobster need crutches?

A: It pulled a mussel.

Q: Why did the book have to go to the hospital?

A: To have its appendix removed.

Jim: I want to build a gigantic boat, but I'll need some help.

Bob: Well, I just happen to Noah guy.

Q: When is a noodle a fake?

A: When it's an im-pasta.

Q: What has four legs but can't walk?

A: A chair.

Q: Why do silent frogs live forever?

A: Because they never croak!

Tammy: I'm embarrassed to go to the eye doctor.

Tommy: Why?

Tammy: My doctor always makes a spectacle of himself!

Q: How does a bumblebee stay out of trouble?

A: It stays on its best bee-havior.

Q: When does a hot dog get on your nerves?

A: When it's being a brat—it's the wurst.

Jimmy: Did you hear about the kid that got hit in the head with a can of pop?

Bobby: No, is he ok?

Jimmy: Yep, he's just lucky it was a soft drink.

Emma: I'm reading a book about gravity.

Leah: That's cool. Is it a good book?

Emma: It sure is! I just can't put it down.

Q: Why did the boy stop using his pencil?

A: It was pointless.

Q: Why did the ruler have a bad report card?

A: His grades just didn't measure up.

Q: Why did the wood fall asleep?

A: It was board.

Q: What do you get when you cross a train with a tissue?

A: An achoo-choo train.

Q: Why did the bee need to take allergy medicine?

A: It had lots of hives.

Q: What happens when strawberries are sad?

A: They become blueberries!

Q: What did the judge say to the skunk?

A: "Odor in the court!"

Q: Why was the potato chip mad at the pretzel?

A: Because it was insalting him.

Q: Why can you trust your secrets with a sea lion?

A: Their lips are always seal-ed!

Q: What did the lipstick say to the eye shadow?

A: "We should stop fighting and make-up!"

Q: Where do astronauts keep their sandwiches?

A: In their launch-box.

Q: Why was the man upset after he became a vegetarian?

A: He realized he'd made a missed-steak.

Sam: Did you like that story about the farm?

Sue: No, it didn't have a very good plot.

Q: Why couldn't the Cyclops family get along?

A: They could never see eye-to-eye.

Knock knock.
Who's there?
Bat.
Bat who?
I bat you want to hear some more knock-knock jokes!

Q: What did the shovel say to the sand?

A: "I really dig you!"

Q: Who helps pigs fall in love?

A: Cu-pig.

Q: How do bees get to school?

A: They take the school buzz.

Q: Why can't you tell a joke to an egg?

A: It might crack up!

Q: Why didn't the two 4's come to the dinner table?

A: Because they already 8.

Q: Why was the carpenter mad that he hit the nail with his hammer?

A: Because it was his fingernail!

Knock knock.

Who's there?

Bach.

Bach who?

I'll be Bach later when you're ready to open the door!

Knock knock.

Who's there?

Lasagna.

Lasagna who?

Are you going to lasagna couch all day, or are you going to answer the door?

Knock knock.

Who's there?

Snow.

Snow who?

What, don't you snow me?

Knock knock.

Who's there?

Bacon.

Bacon who?

Don't go bacon my heart.

Q: What kind of bugs like to sneak up on you?

A: Spy-ders.

Q: What do magicians like to eat for breakfast?

A: Trix cereal.

Knock knock.

Who's there?

Shore.

Shore who?

I shore hope you know some more knock-knock jokes!

Knock knock.

Who's there?

Minnow.

Minnow who?

Let minnow when you plan on letting me in!

Q: What kind of cars do deep-sea divers drive?

A: Scubarus.

Q: What is a whale's motto?

A: "Seas the Day."

Q: Why did the shoe fall in love with the boot?

A: Because they were sole mates.

Knock knock.

Who's there?

Roach.

Roach who?

I roach you a letter—will you write back soon?

Q: Why was the snail moving so slow?

A: It was feeling sluggish.

Q: Why did the frog get sent home from school?

A: He was a bully-frog!

Q: What happened when they invented the broom?

A: It was an idea that swept the nation!

Q: How does Moses make his tea?

A: Hebrews it.

Q: Why do cows wear cowbells?

A: Because they don't have horns.

Q: **What kind of dogs are always on time?**

A: Watch dogs!

Q: **What is the best way to communicate with a fish?**

A: Drop it a line.

Q: **How does Jack Frost get around?**

A: On his motor-cicle.

Q: **What do you get when you cross a bear and a pig?**

A: A grizzly boar!

Q: **When should you stay away from a comedian?**

A: When they want to give you the punch-line!

Q: **How did the marching band keep their teeth clean?**

A: With a tuba toothpaste.

Q: **Why wouldn't the lions play games with the zebras?**

A: There were too many cheetahs.

Q: **How do comedians like their eggs?**

A: Funny-side up.

Knock knock.

Who's there?

Moe.

Moe who?

Do you know any Moe knock-knock jokes?

Q: Why is the ocean so much fun?

A: You can always have a whale of a time.

Q: When can't you believe anything a hippo-potamus says?

A: When it's a hippo-crite.

Knock knock.

Who's there?

Taco.

Taco who?

I don't want to taco 'bout it—just let me in!

Q: **What did the violin say to the guitar when it was worried?**

A: "Don't fret!"

Q: **Why are omelets so out of shape?**

A: They don't get enough eggs-ercise.

Q: **Why didn't the cow have any money?**

A: The farmer had milked it for all its worth!

Peter: You have got to put pickles on your sandwich!

Penny: Why, what's the big dill?

Q: What did the C note say to the D note?

A: "Stop! You're under a rest."

Q: How do you know if your printer likes music?

A: When it's always jamming.

Knock knock.

Who's there?

Bacon.

Bacon who?

Let me in—I'm bacon out here!

Q: Where do cows go on the weekends?

A: To the moo-seum.

Q: When does a king have trouble breathing?

A: When he doesn't have any heir.

Q: What do you give a deer with a tummy ache?

A: Elk-aseltzer.

Q: Why did the bear eat a lamp?

A: It just wanted a light snack.

Q: Where did the beaver put its money?

A: In the river bank.

Q: Why did the house go to the doctor?

A: It had a lot of window panes.

Q: Why was the bee's hair all sticky?

A: It used a honeycomb.

Q: What do you get when you try a new kind of bread for the first time?

A: Meet-loaf.

Q: Why did the police arrest the chicken?

A: They suspected fowl play.

Knock knock.
>Who's there?

Isaac.
>Isaac who?

Isaac of these knock-knock jokes!

Q: What is a frisbee's favorite kind of music?

A: Disk-o.

Q: Why wouldn't the worm buy anything new?

A: It was dirt cheap.

Sue: Did you hear about the towel
that liked to tell jokes?

Alley: Was the towel funny?

Sue: It had a dry sense of humor.

Q: Why did the pig have to sit on the bench
during football practice?

A: He pulled his ham-string.

Q: What is a good thing to eat when you're
feeling stressed?

A: A marsh-mellow.

Q: What kind of shoes do bakers wear?

A: Loaf-ers.

Q: **What did the orange say when it was stepped on?**

A: You hurt my peelings!

Q: **Why were all the animals laughing at the owl?**

A: Because he was a hoot!

Q: **What do you get when you combine a monster and a genius?**

A: Frank-Einstein.

Q: **Why couldn't all the king's horses and all the king's men put Humpty Dumpty together again?**

A: They were eggshausted.

Q: What did the composer say after the symphony?

A: "I'll be Bach."

Q: What do frogs eat on a really hot day?

A: Hop-sicles.

Q: Why did the boy always carry his piggy bank outside?

A: In case there was change in the weather.

Q: Why was the math teacher sad?

A: He had a lot of problems to solve.

Q: How did the police know the invisible
man was lying?

A: They could see right through him.

Q: Why did the cat like to go bowling?

A: It was an alley cat.

Q: Why do basketball players need so many
napkins?

A: They're always dribbling!

Q: Why did the bird go to the hospital?

A: To get medical tweetment.

Q: Why did the monkey go to the golf course?

A: So it could practice its swing.

Q: Where do bees go when they get married?

A: On their honey-moon.

Q: What do you call a bear with no socks?

A: Bear-foot.

Q: When can't you trust a farmer?

A: When he spills the beans!

Q: What do you call a cowboy that falls off his horse?

A: An OW-boy!

Q: Where do ducks live in the city?

A: In their pond-ominiums.

Q: What kind of animal has the best eyesight?

A: A see lion.

Q: How did the tuba call the trumpet?

A: On his saxo-phone.

Q: What do you call a really big insect?

A: A gi-ant.

Q: How did the barber win the race?

A: He took a short-cut.

Q: Where do polar bears go to vote?

A: The North Poll.

Q: What did the baby corn say to the mommy corn?

A: "Where is Pop-corn?"

Knock knock.

Who's there?

Lava.

Lava who?

I lava you!

Q: **What do bumblebees play at the park?**

A: Fris-bee.

Q: **Why do gorillas have big fingers?**

A: Because they have big nostrils.

Q: **What did the doe say to the fawn when it was naughty?**

A: "The buck stops here!"

Q: Why are sheep so gullible?

A: It's easy to pull the wool over their eyes.

Q: What did the hat say to the scarf?

A: "You hang around here for a while—I'm going to go ahead."

Q: When does the alphabet only have 24 letters?

A: When U and I are not part of it!

Q: What kind of photographs do dentists take?

A: Tooth pics.

Q: When is a dinosaur boring to hang around with?

A: When it's a dino-snore.

Q: What happened to the cow when it lost its GPS?

A: It became udderly lost!

Vicki: Do you want to hear my joke about pizza?

Leah: Not really!

Vicki: Well, it was kind of cheesy anyway!

Knock knock.

Who's there?

Owl.

Owl who?

Owl wait right here until you open the door!

Q: How do clams call home?

A: They use their shell phones!

Q: What do monsters sing at the ball game?

A: The national phantom.

Q: Why can't you invite pigs to your birthday party?

A: They might go hog wild.

Q: What do frogs wear in the summer time?

A: Open-toad shoes.

Q: What kind of sea creature needs help at school?

A: A "C" horse.

Q: What do you find at the end of everything?

A: The letter "g."

Q: What's brown and sticky?

A: A stick.

Q: Why are there frogs on the baseball team?

A: To catch the fly balls!

Samantha: Who stole the poor baby octopus?

Henry: I don't know, who?

Samantha: The squidnappers!

Q: What do snowmen like best at school?

A: Snow and tell.

Q: What do you get from grumpy cows?

A: Sour milk!

Knock knock.

Who's there?

Yam.

Yam who?

I yam glad you asked—it's me!

Justin: I had a terrible dream about horses last night.

Anna: Was it a night-mare?

Q: What do music and chickens have in common?

A: Bach, Bach, Bach!

Q: Why can't you win a race with a rope?

A: It will always end with a tie.

Knock knock.

Who's there?

Butter.

Butter who?

I butter tell you a few more knock-knock jokes.

Q: Why should you always be nice to a horse?

A: Because you should love your neigh-bor as yourself.

Q: Why don't you want to fight with a snail?

A: It might try to slug you.

Knock knock.

Who's there?

Grape.

Grape who?

It would be grape if you'd tell me some more knock-knock jokes!

Q: Where does a shark go on Saturday nights?

A: To the dive-in movies.

Q: What did the girl oyster say to the boy oyster?

A: "You always clam up when I try to talk to you!"

Q: Why can't you win an argument with a pencil?

A: It's always write.

Q: What animal can jump higher than a house?

A: All of them—houses can't jump!

Q: Why couldn't the skunk go to shopping?

A: It didn't have a scent in its wallet.

Q: Why did the boat go to the mall?

A: It was looking for a sail.

Q: Should we use a rowboat or a canoe to get across the lake?

A: It's either-oar.

Q: What has 50 feet and sings?

A: A choir.

Q: What do you call a cow with two legs?

A: Lean beef.

Knock knock.

Who's there?

Whale.

Whale who?

Whale you tell me another knock-knock joke?

Knock knock.

Who's there?

Gouda.

Gouda who?

Tell me another gouda knock-knock joke.

Q: Why did the people pucker up every time they drove around town?

A: Because they were driving a lemon!

Q: How can you learn more about spiders?

A: Check out their web-site.

Q: What do you call a guy stuffed in your mailbox?

A: Bill.

Josh: How do you know that eating carrots is good for your eyes?

John: Well, have you ever seen a rabbit with glasses before?

Margie: Would you like to go camping this weekend?

Minnie: No, that sounds too in-tents for me.

Q: What happens when you cross a river and a stream?

A: You get wet feet!

Q: What is smarter than a talking cat?

A: A spelling bee.

Q: Why did the bunny go to the hospital?

A: It needed a hop-eration.

Q: Why did the reporter go to the ice cream parlor?

A: He wanted to get the scoop!

Q: What is a drummer's favorite vegetable?

A: A beet.

Q: Why is it hard to carry on a conversation with rams?

A: Because they're always butting in!

Q: What kind of bear stays out in the rain?

A: A drizzly bear.

Knock knock.

Who's there?

Bean.

Bean who?

I've bean waiting for you to open the door!

Knock knock.

Who's there?

Porpoise.

Porpoise who?

Are you leaving me out here on porpoise or will you answer the door?

Knock knock.

Who's there?

Wyatt.

Wyatt who?

Wyatt is taking you so long to open the door?

Knock knock.

Who's there?

Dawn.

Dawn who?

It just Dawn-ed on me—I should tell another knock-knock joke!

Q: Why did the duck set his alarm for so early in the morning?

A: He liked to get up at the quack of dawn!

Q: What do you call a skeleton that isn't very smart?

A: A numbskull.

Q: What do you get when you cross a daisy and a bike?

A: Bicycle petals.

Knock knock.

Who's there?

Cook.

Cook who?

You sound a little crazy!

Knock knock.

Who's there?

Harry.

Harry who?

Harry up and answer the door, and I'll tell you another joke!

Q: Where can you learn to make ice cream treats?

A: In sundae school.

Q: Why don't math books last very long?

A: Their days are numbered.

Knock knock.

Who's there?

Nose.

Nose who?

Nobody nose a good joke when they hear one anymore!

Q: What do computer programmers eat when they're hungry?

A: Bytes of chips.

Q: Where do mermaids go for fun?

A: The dive-in movies!

Q: What kind of bird has a lot of money?

A: An ost-rich.

Q: **Where is the best place to keep an angry dog?**

A: In the grrrrage.

Q: **What kind of coat is always wet and colorful?**

A: A coat of paint!

Q: **Why did the bat join the circus?**

A: So it could be an acro-bat.

Knock knock.

Who's there?

Wheel.

Wheel who?

Wheel you let me tell you another knock-knock joke?

Knock knock.

Who's there?

Mark Twain.

Mark Twain who?

You mark my words, the twain will be here soon!

Q: What kind of shoes do monsters wear?

A: Combat boo-ts!

Q: What do garbage collectors eat for lunch?

A: Junk food!

Q: What kind of bird always shows up at dinnertime?

A: A swallow.

Q: What's a lion's favorite day of the week?

A: Chewsday.

Q: How do elk know it's hunting season?

A: They check their calen-deer!

Q: What did the snowman say to Jack Frost?

A: "Have an ice day!"

Q: What is a golfer's favorite drink?

A: Iced tee.

Q: What do you wear to play mini-golf?

A: A tee-shirt.

Q: How do porcupines stay warm in the winter?

A: They cover up with a quill-t!

Q: What kind of dogs chop down trees?

A: Lumber Jack Russells.

Knock knock.
   Who's there?
Turnip.
   Turnip who?
Turnip the heat—it's cold out here!

Q: What kind of cars do monsters drive?

A: Doom buggies.

Q: What did the lamb want to
be when she grew up?

A: A baaaa-llerina.

Q: How can you tell when a bell is old?

A: It has ring-kles.

Q: What did the cell phone say to the
landline?

A: "Hi, Grandma!"

Q: What is a rat's favorite website?

A: Mice-space.

Q: What does a clam wear to the gym?

A: A mussel shirt.

Q: Why did the snake cross the road?

A: To get to the other sssssss-ide!

Q: What is the cleanest state?

A: Wash-ington!

Knock knock.

Who's there?

Water.

Water who?

Water you doing later?

Q: What's black and white and goes around, around, and around?

A: A penguin stuck in a revolving door!

Q: Why do penguins carry fish in their beaks?

A: They don't have any pockets.

Q: What do you get when you put your notebook in your bed?

A: Sheets of paper!

Q: What do you get when you step on a piano?

A: Foot-notes!

Q: How does the snowman like his root beer?

A: In a frosted mug.

Q: What does Jack Frost call his parents?

A: Mom and Pop-sicle!

Q: Why did Frosty go live in the middle of the ocean?

A: Because snow man is an island!

tongue twisters

Irish wristwatch, Swiss wristwatch

Plump pink pillows

Splish splash plip plop

Coloring with crayons can cause cramps

Spunky pumpkins

Good bread, bad bread

Bouncy blue beach balls

Tickling tiny turkey toes

Crispy kitty cookies

Q: What do you get when you hang a trumpet on a Christmas tree?

A: A Christmas hornament.

Q: How do crocodiles like to cook their food?

A: In a crockpot!

Knock knock.

Who's there?

Window.

Window who?

Window we get to hear another knock-knock joke?

Wade: What do you think of my rash?

Merv: It's kind of gross.

Wade: Just wait a while—it will grow on you!

Q: Why are possums so lazy?

A: All they do is hang around.

Q: Why did the billboard go to the doctor?

A: It had a sign-us infection.

Q: What do you say to a noisy jar?

A: "Put a lid on it!"

Q: What do you get when you cross a cow and a rabbit?

A: Hare in your milk!

Q: What do get when you borrow money from a cow?

A: A buffa-loan.

Knock knock.
Who's there?
Cheryl.
Cheryl who?
Cheryl be glad to tell you another knock-knock joke!

Q: What does a carpenter eat for lunch?

A: A ham-mer and cheese sandwich.

Q: What happens when you throw your vegetables in the ocean?

A: You get sea cucumbers!

Q: Why was the cow embarrassed?

A: It had become a laughing stock.

Q: Where do musicians like to kiss?

A: Under the mistle-tone.

Q: What did the fork say to the knife?

A: "No need to be so blunt!"

Q: Why wouldn't anyone talk to the bread?

A: It was a weir-dough.

Q: Where does a horse go when it's sick?

A: To the horse-pital.

Knock knock.
  Who's there?
Ache.
  Ache who?
God bless you!

Q: What happened after the man accidently dropped his coffee in the volcano?

A: Java came out!

Q: What did the pen say to the pencil?

A: "Get the lead out!"

Q: **What do skunks sing at Christmas time?**

A: Jingle smells, jingle smells.

Q: **Why did the calendar have such a great attitude?**

A: It was taking life one day at a time!

Knock knock.

Who's there?

Owl.

Owl who?

I'm owl by myself, please let me in.

Q: **Why was the bird always crying?**

A: Because it was a blue bird!

Q: What do bugs need to do their homework?

A: An ant-cyclopedia.

Q: What do you get when you combine an elephant and an insect?

A: An eleph-ant.

Q: What did the bread say to the baker?

A: "I need you to knead me."

Q: Why was the skeleton laughing?

A: Because he found his humerus.

Knock knock.

Who's there?

Token.

Token who?

Now that's what I'm token about!

Q: **What do frogs order when they go to fast food restaurants?**

A: French flies and croak-a-cola.

Anna: **Was that a skeleton at the door?**

Leah: No, it was no body.

Q: **Why was the whale always bragging?**

A: Because it was fishing for compliments.

Q: What do black bears wear in their hair?

A: Bearrettes.

Q: What kind of fish comes out at night?

A: A starfish.

Q: What makes bananas such great drivers?

A: They're always keeping their eyes peeled.

Q: What did the mouse say to the rat at the movies?

A: "The squeakuel is never as good as the original."

Q: Why is jelly always so much fun?

A: Because it's always jamming.

Q: Why was the sheep practicing karate?

A: Because it was a lamb chop!

Q: What kind of clothing do disobedient children wear?

A: They wear smarty-pants.

Q: Where do fish get their money?

A: From the loan shark.

Q: How do ants cook their food?

A: With a micro-wave!

Q: How do you have a party on Mars?

A: You have to planet.

Rob Elliott has been a publishing professional for more than twenty years and lives in West Michigan, where in his spare time he enjoys laughing out loud with his wife and four children.

Need More Laughs?

‒ ‒ ‒ ‒ ‒ ‒ ‒ * ‒ ‒ ‒ ‒ ‒ ‒ ‒

Visit

LOLJokesForKids.com

to submit your own jokes,
receive FREE printable doodle pages,
and watch the video!

• • •

Laugh-Out-Loud Jokes for Kids

@loljokesforkids

Collect them all!

Doodles for
Everyone!

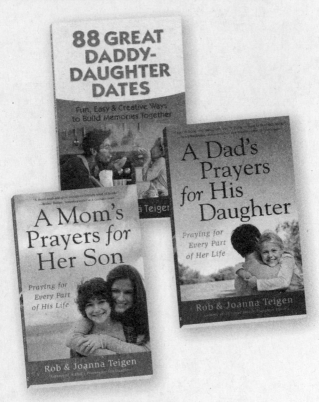